I0151857

HOW TO BE COURAGEOUS

Information and Encouragement with Inspirational Short Stories by Teens and Young Adults

Jennifer Leigh Youngs, A.A. · Bettie B. Youngs, Ph.D., Ed.D.

from the SMART TEENS-SMART CHOICES series

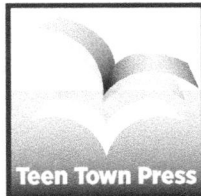

Teen Town Press

Teen Town Press
www.TeenTownPress.com

an imprint of Bettie Youngs Book Publishers, Inc.

BB
BETTIE YOUNGS BOOKS

Cover Graphic Design: Adrian Pitariu and Beau Kimbrel
Text Design: Beau Kimbrel
Teen Consultant: Kendahl Brooke Youngs

TEEN TOWN PRESS / www.TeenTownPress.com is an Imprint of Bettie Youngs Book Publishing Co., Inc.: www.BettieYoungsBooks.com; info@BettieYoungsBooks.com.

If you are unable to order this book from your local bookseller or online, or Ingram Book Group, you may order directly from the publisher: info@BettieYoungsBooks.com.

PRINT ISBN: 978-1-940784-93-9
DIGITAL ISBN: 978-1-940784-92-2

10 9 8 7 6 5 4 3 2

Library of Congress Cataloging-in-Publication Data Available upon Request.

Summary: information and encouragement and inspirational short stories by teens and young adults showing courage in everyday life.
1. YAN literature. 2. Values. 3. Virtues. 4. Teens and Young Adults.
5. Courage. 6. Confidence. 7. Self-Reliance. 8. Self-efficacy.
9. Youngs, Bettie Burres. 10. Youngs, Jennifer Leigh.
11. Youngs, Kendahl Brooke.

Also by the Authors for Teens and Young Adults

How Your Brain Decides If You Will Become Addicted—Or Not

Setting and Achieving Goals that Matter TO ME

Managing the Stress, Pressure and the Ups and Downs of Life

The 10 Commandments and the Secret Each One Guards—FOR YOU

How to Be Courageous

Growing Your Confidence and Self-Esteem

Faith at Work in Our Lives

Understanding Feelings of Love

Understanding the Christian Faith

How to be a Good Friend

Having Healthy and Beautiful Hair, Skin and Nails

The Power of Being Kind, Courteous and Thoughtful

How to Have a Great Attitude

Caring for Your Body's Health and Wellness

Daily Inspiration

Inspirational Stories and Encouragement on Friends and the Face in the Mirror

CONTENTS

   - Integrity and Self-Discipline
   - Doing the Right Thing
   - Knowing Your Values
   - Being a Hero

OTHER BOOKS BY THE AUTHORS

CHAPTER 1

COURAGE:
We're All Heroes in the Making

Courage is the first and foremost of all qualities, because it is the one upon which all others depend.
—Winston Churchill

From the French word Coeur, meaning heart, courage is, as Winston Churchill (England's courageous leader during World War II) once said, *"The first and foremost of all qualities, because it is the one upon which all others depend."*

All emotions, all behavior, and strength of character require great heart. Courage is the first and most important "ingredient" determining our willingness and ability—our readiness and determination—to act with conviction, and in positive, loving and responsible ways.

Courage: What a powerful word; just hearing it evokes a sense of strength. But what is courage, and what does it take to be courageous? We often think of groups for their bravery, such as soldiers, firefighters or others who often put their lives on the line in helping others, as courageous. While many consider courage to be a positive quality, many think it is attained by only chosen few. But courage is not an elusive quality. Nor is it out of reach for you and me. We are all heroes in the making!

Think of three people you consider courageous who you know personally. Who comes to mind? Are you courageous? Do you consider yourself to be one of the most courageous people you know?

> Courage is not an elusive quality.
> We are all heroes in the making!

Courage is a Muscle

It's been said that courage is a "muscle" and that the more you act in courageous ways, the more you develop courage.

Do you believe that? Do you think courage is innate—that we are born with various degrees of it—which then would explain why some people seem to be more "courageous" than others? Or is courage a trait that can readily be developed—and so those who act in courageous ways become "people of courage"?

> A person develops courage by doing
> courageous acts.
> —**Aristotle**

In the stories by teens and young adults throughout this book, you'll get a chance to see the many ways courage shows up in our lives, and the "price" of courage. Do you want to experience love? If so, then you must also risk heartbreak. What about friendship? Yes, if you put yourself out there to make friends, you also must risk rejection and maybe even betrayal, and loss of friendship, too.

Courage is needed in all that we do. Does that mean that it comes without fear? No. Courage is not the absence of fear. Courage is doing something because to you, it is the right thing to do.

> Courage is not the absence of fear.
> Courage is doing what needs to be done
> despite the fear.

We all experience fear. But those who live life with great heart—courage—make the decision to not let their fears stop them. A great basketball player for the Boston Celtics, Bill Russell, said that he became so nervous before basketball games that he threw up! His fear didn't stop him from becoming a world champion eight times and one of the greatest centers to ever play the game.

Fear is a useful emotion. It alerts us to take action. And, it warns us of danger. It says, "There is a risk here, so be careful or turn back." This can save us from a lot of trouble, even save our lives.

Sometimes we have too little fear, and we foolishly rush into situations that we should avoid. That's why it's important to listen to our instincts and intuition before we jump.

We must ask ourselves: What is the risk here and what is my purpose in taking this risk? For example, people who do drugs for a dare are often unaware of the real risks; they aren't being courageous, only reckless.

8 WAYS TO HAVE EVERYDAY COURAGE

While courage can mean we must rise to the challenge of an extraordinary feat that takes a great deal of physical stamina or emotional fortitude, it can also be subtle. Sometimes we may not even be aware that what we did or said was an act of courage.

Courage can take many forms.

EMOTIONAL COURAGE. It is easy to see how we need courage when dealing with physical challenges but handling our emotions can take just as much courage. As fifteen-year-old Cecily explained, *"When Aaron dumped me, I was crushed. We had been dating almost a whole year, and I really loved him a lot. When he announced that he 'had feelings' for someone else, I thought I would be sick. I felt like never going back to the same school again. And I was down on love: I* *just knew I never wanted to ever get that close to someone again. But I had to go to school anyway. It was so difficult, and so painful. But I did it. And I'm okay now. My heart hurts less and less when I see him. I'm not going let this ruin my entire year, and I'm going to risk liking a new boy when the time is right."*

Coping with heartache and pain does take emotional courage. When we allow ourselves to be vulnerable to others, when we open ourselves to the fun and happiness of love and friendship, those opportunities also carry with them the risk of rejection and loss.

THE COURAGE TO RISK FAILURE. A willingness to try, knowing that you may fail, takes courage but without this courage, you might not try new things, and lose the chance to grow in the process. As 13-year-old Erica explained, *"I really wanted a part in the school play, but there were so many girls trying out that I didn't think I had a chance, even though everybody told me I had a really good voice and all. I just kept making up excuses, so I didn't have to face the possibility of losing out. Then when this girl got the lead—someone who really wasn't much better than me—I realized I could have gotten a pretty good part even if I didn't get the lead. Besides, all my friends who just got into the chorus seemed to have a great time just being in the play. I wish I wasn't so afraid of trying sometimes."*

It's better to try and fail than not try at all. Everyone experiences failure. The goal is to believe you can learn from your failures how to be better next time, and keep improving.

THE COURAGE TO ACCEPT OURSELVES. It takes much courage to accept ourselves, flaws and all. As Rebecca Lane tells it, *"I am a big-boned girl. My mother is nearly six feet tall, and my father is six-feet-four. I'm fifteen and stand five-eleven. I weigh 150 pounds. Because I tower over many of the kids in my school, others take a lot of potshots at me. It takes a great deal of courage for me to stand tall and take their ridiculing in a good-natured way, as opposed to being really upset and even rude in return. But I've made that choice to say basically, 'Hey, this is me, and I like it.' I've decided to accept myself, and not fall for taunts."*

Unfortunately "body-shaming" is all too prevalent for young people. It's good to see that Rebecca has opted for courage to stand tall in the face of taunts from her classmates. It's good to see that she has made friends with the face in the mirror, and allows that voice (her own) to reign.

THE COURAGE TO PERSEVERE. The courage to keep going even when the going gets tough, whether in school, with friends, on the job or in sports or whenever you need to stand tall for yourself, shows perseverance. It's the "keep on, keeping on."

Abraham Lincoln lost sixteen elections before becoming president. And Steve Smith, a most well-respected astronaut—veteran of two space flights, more than three hundred Earth orbits, and three space walks—tried out a total of five times before he succeeded in earning his coveted spot as an American astronaut. Julie Mayor failed to make the cut for the U.S. Olympic Soccer Team three times, but that didn't stop her from trying yet a fourth time. Today, Julie Mayor is an Olympic gold medalist.

What if Lincoln, Steve and Julie had given up the first (or second or third!) time they failed in their attempts to reach their respective goals? If you want to succeed, you must have the courage to persevere.

THE COURAGE TO CHANGE. We sometimes get comfortable with what is familiar, even if that doesn't produce a good result, such as a bad habit. It takes courage to change. The courage to change our approach, our attitudes, even ourselves, means we have to dig deep and accept that sometimes change is necessary, as was the case for McKenzy Jean's friend who had a bad habit of always being late.

THE COURAGE TO DELAY OUR GRATIFICATION. The slogan of a two-year-old is "I want what I want when I want it." As Oscar Wilde once joked, "I can resist anything but temptation." Part of maturing is learning that things don't always come easy, nor instantly. It takes courage to delay gratification when you want what you want, sooner than later. Teaching yourself to be patient takes great courage.

THE COURAGE OF YOUR CONVICTIONS. Doing what you believe is right, even when it is not always easy or convenient to do so, is an act of courage. If you stand up to those who are teasing someone even though they may put you down as well, if you believe that cheating is wrong so you don't cheat even though someone else is, such conviction is an act of courage. It is easy to say you have a conviction that is "honorable and just," but having the character to put those convictions into action takes courage.

THE COURAGE TO DO WHAT IS RIGHT, ALL THE TIME. When others, even friends, are going in a direction that you know in your heart is wrong, or at least wrong for you, the peer pressure to go with the flow of the crowd is tempting. Following your moral compass is important. It takes courage to stand up and go the right way, even if you're the only one going in that direction.

> Life is a journey filled with lessons in developing courage: have heart, and live fully. This helps you trust the wind beneath your wings.

Life is a journey filled with lessons in developing courage! See yourself as a hero (or heroine) in-the-making. Living with integrity takes great heart and great courage. But when we do that, it gives others the courage to do the same.

CHAPTER 2
The Attributes of Courage

Courage is resilience to fear, mastery of fear, not absence of fear.

—**Mark Twain**

The fear that accompanies *physical courage* can be about worrying if you are physically strong enough to confront whatever is making you fearful, such as fleeing from, or, facing down a snarling dog.

Moral courage compels or allows an individual to do what he or she believes is right, despite fear of the consequences. What is "right" is determined by the person who chooses to take the action chosen.

Courage is not only physical bravery. Social activists, such as Martin Luther King and Nelson Mandela—who chose to speak out against injustice—or entrepreneurs such as Steve Jobs and Walt Disney—who took financial risks to follow their *dreams* and innovate—are all courageous. There are different types of courage, ranging from physical strength and endurance to mental stamina and *innovation*, and others, too.

The following quotes speak to different ways to define courage.

Feeling Fear, Yet Choosing to Act

❤ *Fear and courage are brothers.* —Proverb

❤ I learned that courage was not the absence of fear, but the triumph over it. The brave man is not he who does not feel afraid, but he who conquers that fear. —Nelson Mandela

❤ There is no living thing that is not afraid when it faces danger. The true courage is in facing danger when you are afraid. —L. Frank Baum, *The Wonderful Wizard of Oz*

❤ The one who feels no fear is a fool, and the one who lets fear rule him is a coward.

—Piers Anthony

❤ Courage is about doing what you're afraid to do. There can be no courage unless you're scared. Have the courage to act instead of react. —Oliver Wendell Holmes

Following Your Heart

❤ Passion is what drives us crazy, what makes us do extraordinary things, to discover, to challenge ourselves. Passion is and should always be the heart of courage.

—Midori Komatsu

❤ Have the courage to follow your heart and intuition. They somehow already know what you truly want to become. Everything else is secondary. —Steve Jobs, Stanford University commencement speech

❤ To dare is to lose one's footing momentarily. To not dare is to lose oneself.

— Soren Kierkegaard

❤ It takes courage . . . to endure the sharp pains of self-discovery rather than choose to take the dull pain of unconsciousness that would last the rest of our lives. —Marianne Williamson, "Return to Love: Reflections on the Principles of 'A Comse in Miracles'"

Persevering in the Face of Adversity

❤ A hero is no braver than an ordinary man, but he is braver five minutes longer.

—Ralph Waldo Emerson (1803-1882)

❤ Most of our obstacles would melt away if, instead of cowering before them, we should make up our minds to walk boldly through them. —Orison Swett Marden (1850-1924)

❤ Courage doesn't always roar. Sometimes courage is the little voice at the end of the day that says "I'll try again tomorrow."

—Mary Anne Radmacher

❤ It's not the size of the dog in the fight, it's the size of the fight in the dog. —Mark Twain

---

Standing Up for What Is Right

❤ Sometimes standing against evil is more important than defeating it. The greatest heroes stand because it is right to do so, not because they believe they will walk away with their lives. Such selfless courage is a victory in itself —N. D. Wilson, Dandelion Fire

❤ Speak your mind, even if your voice shakes.
　　　　　　—Maggie Kuhn, Social Activist

❤ From caring comes courage. —Lao Tzu

Expanding Your Horizons; Moving On

❤ Man cannot discover new oceans unless he has the courage to lose sight of the shore.
　　　　　　—Lord Chesterfield

❤ This world demands the qualities of youth; not a time of life but a state of mind, a temper of the will, a quality of the imagination, a predominance of courage over timidity, of the appetite for adventure over the life of ease.
　　　　　　—Robert F. Kennedy

❤ Life shrinks or expands in proportion to one's courage. —Anais Nin

---

Facing Suffering With
Dignity and Grace . . .

❤ There is no need to be ashamed of tears, for tears bear witness that a man has the greatest of courage, the courage to suffer.

—Viktor Frankl

❤ The ideal man bears the accidents of life with dignity and grace, making the best of circumstances. —Aristotle

❤ Until the day of his death, no man can be sure of his courage. —Jean Anoulh

❤ A man of courage is also full of faith.

—Marcus Tullius Cicero

Of all these quotes, which is your most favorite, and why?

_____

_____

_____

Courage-Building Exercise

Write aboutf a situation you are currently facing that creates fear or *anxiety*.

_____

_____

_____

Now think about what you can do to face the fear and move through it. For example: John has a friend who is also his locker mate, who steals things from others, and John is wanting to tell him to stop. But, John is afraid he'll then take things he keeps in the locker they share.

How can you handle your situation? The goal is to see yourself as growing in your willingness and ability to be a courageous person.

_____

_____

_____

_____

CHAPTER 3

Stories About Courage by Teens and Young Adults

In the following stories you'll get a chance to see how others grew their courage. Sometimes this meant overcoming a hurdle or a discouraging time. Have you ever been discouraged? Most all of us have. It's important to know that we can all learn how to turn that around and important that we do. Negative thinking is often paralyzing and leads to feeling even more discouraged. This creates more negative thinking and more discouragement.

Positive thinking helps generate the courage to improve and make things work. These successes generate more positive thinking and more courage. You become encouraged. There is a saying that "nothing succeeds like success." This means that when we start having successes in our lives, we often have more successes. The reason is that we become encouraged to try harder, and handle mistakes and setbacks in stride without giving up.

How do you stay encouraged and not discouraged? The first step is to encourage yourself. You build courage when you use challenges, tough times and discouraging moments as opportunities to cope, to manage your emotions, to do positive self-talk, to walk through these times.

You are a hero-in-the-making. Think of yourself as a courageous person, as the teens in the following stories are learning to do.

An Acrophobic's "Plunge"

From here on out, I'm going to "go for it!" I was put on this planet to live, not just breathe.
—Mike Siciliano, 17

"Go ahead, jump!" a buddy of mine taunted, and then dared, "Bet you won't!" I looked into the water from where I was standing and knew he was probably right. Standing practically on top of the world—at least it felt that way to me—and thinking of plunging into the depths of an endless ocean below, I was scared to death! I'm an acrophobic (I have a fear of heights), so you can imagine the chill that went down my spine as I considered the possibilities of taking up the dare. I moved closer to the edge of the three-thousand-feet-high platform to take a better look at the distance "down" and began thinking—which is probably the worst thing I could have done.

"You can do it!" one voice coaxed.

"No, you fool! You'll kill yourself!" warned another.

"Oh, go on! Do it!" the first one prodded.

"But I've never done this before!" pleaded the sane voice.

"That's because you always play it safe; find your courage!," mocked the first.

"I can't," assured the second voice.

"C'mon! Don't wimp out—jump!" taunted the

first. (I hate losing to that voice.)

I jumped!

The good news is, I'm alive to tell the story!

Okay, let me tell you that I didn't jump three thousand feet. It was more like three hundred feet. Well, in truth it was thirty feet—but it most definitely felt like three thousand to me. And since I'm setting the record straight, the jump wasn't from the top of the world, but rather from a yacht on which I was a guest. But just so you can empathize, you should know that a crowd of nearly fifty pretty cool kids from various teen organizations stood watching— many of whom were friends and classmates (and one who was a very special girl—if you get what I mean) from my own school! All were looking to see if I'd take the bait of jumping off the yacht and into the water. What could I do?

Even though I didn't want to jump, how does one say "no" when everyone in the whole world is watching? I mean, if I hadn't proven myself as "I can do this, no sweat!" I'd never live it down. I'm sure you know the feeling.

As I stood there looking down into the water, I cannot describe the fear I felt knowing I just had to do it. It seemed more like suicide than heroics to me. I mean, I can swim, so it's not like jumping meant automatic death by drowning, but I really am terrified of heights. I looked down— which momentarily snapped me to my senses— and I backed away. But then I remembered that voice saying, "You always play it safe; find your courage!,'' and something in me just let loose. In a split second, I whirled around, took a ten-foot running start and vaulted into the air!

Here's the thing: The jump was a moment I will never, ever forget. It was absolutely, positively and completely exhilarating. Sailing through midair on my way into a bottomless ocean, it occurred to me that my entire life had been lived with reservation, a holding back. Everything was structured; the clock ruled my life. I lived a boring schedule of predictable activity. Why did I always play it safe? Why wasn't I living more courageously? Living life that way was as useless as using a flashlight in broad daylight. No more.

Sailing through the air on my jump that day, I vowed that from here on out, I was going to "go for it!" I was put on this planet to live, not just breathe. As the ocean grew closer to my face, I realized the difference.

I hit the water.

It was baptizing. I am a changed person. I emerged from the water a different person, and not just because I'd found the courage to jump, but also because in the seconds it took for me to go from the top of the yacht to the water, I discovered how liberating it is to feel "courage." And in that moment, I understood I must live bravely from here on out. Now when I hear a voice inside my head trying to hold me back or limit me, by causing me to doubt myself, or by reminding me of times when I failed at something and so may fail at this attempt, too, I recall the voice that said, Be courageous—jump!" I don't mean to say that I take dangerous risks, but that I have made the decision to be a courageous person. I have decided to "go for it." And that has made all the difference.

I'm happy to report that I'm not as afraid of heights as I once was. I liked the way courage felt. All because of that one jump!

—Mike Siciliano, 17

Curlicue on the Mountain

As a rock climber, there are always certain moments when you're terrified. But when you reach deep down for courage, you move from fear to action, and that's when you discover that Sir Edmund Hillary was right: "It's not just the mountain we conquer, but ourselves."

—Emily Manning, 15

Looking up the mountain, I surveyed the huge cliffs: one enormous boulder overlapping another. All I could manage to say was, "Whoa!" A feeling of sheer terror overcame me, and I quickly ran through my "safety net" check: Whistle, water, phone, flares, patting my pockets to feel these things. I'd come to climb this mountain. Terrified or not, I was going to give it my all. Okay, let's go, I told myself realizing it was now or never!

I just love this sport and being outdoors in nature is one of the many reasons. Most always Mother Nature is "speaking" at the top of her lungs. Today I see vibrant bluebells with their delicate little heads bobbing in the wind; water droplets glittering like jewels on their velvety blue and purple petals; Indian paintbrush bursting with their elaborate fiery red blooms; birds soaring the skies. I scan the panorama, taking in the grandeur. "Grandeur": it's such a great word, one that really describes the view of nature—most especially for me when I'm hanging from a mountain midway up!

I also love rock climbing because it fills me with a sense of courage and power. Nature is so awesome, and "playing in it" makes me feel so honored. Here, in the middle of the mountain, all this beauty is mine for the gazing. I own the sunshine. I own all the sounds around me. In fact, I pretty much own the world! It's a great feeling! Always, I sort of feel like the mountain is happy that I want to climb up on top of its shoulders, knowing that from a certain height and angle I can appreciate Mother Nature even more than by standing amidst it on the ground.

While the surroundings are serene, the sport itself is not what I would describe as tranquil or peaceful. You need all your wits about you when you're doing a climb. But I wouldn't call it nerve-wracking, either. "Exhilarating" best describes it. A little of this has to do with the fact that you are literally hanging off a mountain, and so you literally hold your very life in your own hands. On the mountain, I'm competing with me, and only me. It's a one-on-one challenge: Me taking on ME! Can I do it—well, I'd better, right? There is no sloughing off when you're rock climbing! On the mountain, you'd better be ready to dig deep for courage, because there are times when you need every ounce you can find! Every moment is about looking out for your safety. You are, after all, hanging on a rock cliff!

I also like the feeling of self-reliance. In this sport, even when you go with a group, in the actual climb most moments are spent alone. This is a time when the "It's all about me!" slogan really fits. It is all about me—and not falling! With each step, I learn a lot about myself. In the beginning I had to learn to trust myself in ways I'd never done before. And I had to develop the confidence in myself so that I could trust myself. But once I did, then the world opened to me on a whole new level. And that's when I knew I could do anything! That's when I best learned the meaning of courage. I love that feeling.

On the mountain, I own myself.

Rock climbing also tests your endurance. You must "endure" the climb. In the beginning of it you feel good. Even great. But then a couple of hours later your fingertips are tortured. Your legs are aching and cramped. Your dreams of getting to the top turn to questions of "how." Your confidence turns from "when" to "if." And there is no shortcut. It's a long way up and a longer way down. No point in sitting around. It's up or down.

Now in the middle part of my climb, I look up, knowing I still have a long and steep climb ahead. "Let's go!" I said, urging myself onward and up. Yes, once again I'd accepted the challenge: I would climb Mt. Crested Butte. I continued. One step, and then another. And another. Yet another. Gasping to take in the thinning air. Another step. And another. My water jug tugging at my waist, pleading with me to rest. On I went, taking care not to crush too many cow parsnips or mule's ears, all flowers blooming along the trails. Finally, I saw the boulders, and I knew the steep part of the climb was over. Still, the most treacherous part of the climb was yet to come. A new thrill, a new "high" and more exhilaration. Courage still needed.

Looking down for a foothold among the rocky crevices flipped the world for a moment, but it righted itself when I looked up again. The wind pulling through my hair, I felt like an eagle soaring high with the wind. Suddenly, my right hand slipped and I almost fell, but I grasped a rock just in time. I moved my hand from the unstable rock to a solid handhold and, catching my breath, gazed upward. I had come so far! Only a little more to go. Handhold, foothold, handhold, foothold. It was drilled into my head. Handhold, foothold. Don't fall! Handhold, handhold, handhold. Handhold— where is the handhold? No time for doubts, no room for mistakes. Concentrate. Search for the handhold. Concentrate. Search for the handhold . . . Don't you just love it when an experience brings out the best in you? In this sport we call it "peak performance." Peak performance creates a natural high all its own. It confirms you are courageous.

When I get to the top, I feel as though I've conquered the world! Standing here now, I peek downward and swoon, feeling more than a little dizzy with the height. I look at the town that lay out before me. Rolling hills and streams riddle the landscape. From this view, it looks like a map. Above the town are beautiful mountain peaks, snowcapped peaks with lush green bases. And then I did what I always do when at this point in my climb: I pulled the cap off my Sharpie, and, swelling with pride, signed the log, feeling that with my signature, Mother Nature had just given the mountain to me!

And now for the relaxation part. Lying on the rock, I watched as clouds rolled past and spotted a mountain climber, an elephant, a water jug and a cougar. Interesting mix. Finally, the afternoon sun shone brightly, reminding me that it was time to go home. Enough courage development for today! In the solitude, a single bird chirped, and as it did, I added a final curlicue to my name. It was time to head back down the mountain. My mountain. Sir Edmund Hillary was right: "It's not just the mountain we conquer, but ourselves."

It is during rock climbing that I most understand the nature of courage. For sure, it is when I feel the most courageous.

—Emily Manning, 15

All the Ways He Loved Me

The heart heals faster from surgery than it does from the loss of a loved one.

—Anonymous

Life for me was normal until April 24, 1999, the day my father killed himself.

It's important for me to know that Dad didn't kill himself; the diseases of alcoholism and depression are what killed him. Even with an emphasis on this distinction, his death—and life without him—means my life will never be the same.

Let me first tell you a little about the bright side of my father, a man I loved so much. Dad loved his family and was proud to use the words, "My wife and kids . . ." I am positive that he loved me, and I'm sure my brothers and sisters would say the same. He had many friends. And he was a very successful businessman. Then, there was that dark side of him, one that felt despondent and hopeless to the point that he used alcohol to drown those feelings out. He drowned himself in the process.

When my father died, my first reaction was relief. I know that sounds shocking, but when you live with an alcoholic, life becomes centered on that person's dysfunction—and the stream of stress it creates. It's a relief, a feeling of freedom, to get out from under the blanket of pain and chaos. I remember when, in the first moments I heard the news that my father was dead, there was an immediate knowing that now our family would no longer be imprisoned by the constant worry about Dad's whereabouts—and worrying whether he was alive. As for me personally, now I wouldn't have to experience yet another drinking binge of his, nor worry about when one would occur, or witness and endure his embarrassing behavior in public.

But this sense of relief lasted only for a few moments, when I realized that I'd never see my father again. Never. Not ever. He'd never say, "I love you," again. And I could never tell him to his face that I loved him. Suddenly, there was a deep sadness that my dad would never, ever:

Smile at me
Give me a hug
Help me with homework
Sit in the bleachers at my sports games
Gas up my car (for free) as he always did!
Take pictures of my date and me, or ask me if I
needed a clean shirt to wear
See me graduate from high school—or college
Attend my wedding
Be a grandpa to my children
Be my friend—for life.

With these realizations, a deep sadness set in, knowing how much I'd miss him, and he'd be missed forever. And I felt sorry for myself, and for my mom and brothers, Dad's parents and everyone who loved him.

Next came a boiling anger. Wanting to know, "Why did he do this?" filled my head with the fury of a steaming locomotive. When I wasn't centering this question on the disease that he suffered from, I blamed Dad for abandoning his family and me. It took a lot of courage for me to cast his death in a different light. He "couldn't fix what ailed him"— or at least that's what one of his good friends said at the memorial service.

"The heart heals faster from surgery than it does from the loss of a loved one," a friend of his told me at the memorial service. I could relate: My heart had just undergone emotional triple-bypass surgery— without anesthesia. How would I ever heal?

My first attempt was to put on a strong face, even if my insides were as wobbly as Jell-O. I began the facade the day following the funeral: I'd get up, shower, go to school, and after school, go to baseball practice or hang out with my friends, as usual. Why let my father's inability to handle life stop me from mine? I was going forward.

The strategy pretty much worked except for the fact that my heart wanted nothing more than to withdraw from the world and cry. None of my friends could relate to what I was going through. How could they; their fathers were alive. I'm sure some of them thought I was even better off (they had experienced on many occasions my dad's drunkenness).

Then came another wave of self-pity: Life had been unfair to me! And why me? He was the alcoholic! I had been a good son. Why would he want to leave me and miss out on being with me? And why should I get strapped with life without a dad? All my friends had dads. And judging from all the guilt I went through every minute of every day not to mention the sleepless nights, why should I be suddenly saddled with the stigma of "the kid whose father committed suicide"?

This was followed by yet another stage of anger, one that collapsed into tears and realization: My dad's gone no matter what else—Daddy's gone! I cried myself to sleep and awoke knowing that on April 24, 1999, whether I was ready or not, my life was changed. I had to deal with not having a father and the sad circumstances surrounding his death. I had to deal with myself and the pain his death caused me. I had to deal with thinking about my future, without my father in it. I had to deal with a broken heart and put it back together again.

I'm doing these things. My father's death totally crushed me, but with the help of my mom, friends and faith, I'm finding the courage to rebuild my life. My family and I have been so loving and kind to each other, and that's been helpful. Working with counselors and attending youth group has allowed me to freely talk about my feelings. It helped me let go of the anger and be able to forgive myself for feeling anger toward my father, and to forgive him for the fathering I hadn't received from him (including his not being there in my future). I've come to understand that it was not my father who committed such a desperate act, but rather, the disease from which he suffered.

Now, when I think of my father, I think about how much he loved me and all the ways he showed it:

The smiles
The bear hugs
Helping me with homework
Being at my sports games
Gassing up my car (for free!)
Always taking my picture
Loaning me his shirts...

The list is a long one, and I will always be grateful for his love.

And for the years we had together.

—Kyle Ross, 18

Up to My Neck in Alligators

I've got to find the courage to change.
—Adrian McGhee, 16

My name is Andria McGhee. I'm trying to get my life together. When I was fourteen, I kicked a police officer while being taken to a juvenile detention center. That was just the beginning of my problems; you cannot believe all the grief I've caused myself. When I went to court, the judge flipped through the pages of charges filed against me, and shook his head, and peering over his glasses, "Looks to me as though you're up to your neck in alligators, Miss." Put simply, I've got some jail time ahead me.

I know I've got problems. And I really want to fix them. Like if I don't do something about my bad temper, I'll mess up my life even more than I already have. The first thing I'm going to try to do is to learn how to manage stress. I think that can help me a lot. About the tenth month of being locked up, I had so much stress, especially from thinking about all that I'd done and how long I was going to be locked up because of it, that I got eczema. Eczema is an ugly, scaly and really, itchy rash. Doctors told me I had a "Type-A chronic case." Well, that's for sure: the rash was up and down my entire arms and legs, all over my chest and back, on my stomach and even in my navel. My face was totally covered—and so was my butt. I even had it on my eyelids!

When I stress out, my body starts the rash-reaction thing and I break out. The rash is really an incentive to learn how to manage stress, because when I break out, it itches so bad that sometimes I can't sleep. And if I scratch it, then it gets infected. If it gets infected, it spreads even more. So, it all comes back to my bad temper. What I've learned is that there are consequences to everything. Like if I hadn't been joyriding that day, I wouldn't have been taken to juvenile hall. If I hadn't kicked the officer, I wouldn't have been charged with assault. If I didn't have the charges I do, I wouldn't be facing jail time.

But consequences, I learned, are a two-way street: If I learn how to manage my anger and stress, I can prevent myself from always being up to my neck in alligators. Simply put, I've got to find the courage to change.

—Andria McGhee, 16

Marching Orders from the Heart

How do you find fault with someone for telling you that he needs to break up with you because his heart has made a choice— and it didn't choose you?

—Elizabeth Moria, 17

Alison, my best friend since first grade, dated Nick. He lived nearly two hours away. So that we could double-date, she'd set me up with Nick's best friend, Chris. Though I saw Chris a couple of times, we didn't hit it off, and so we didn't go out again. But Nick and I had feelings for each other right off the bat. We had so much in common. We both had a passion for music, loved to write, and he made me think about things. Conversation between us was easy. He's just a friend, I'd tell myself. But that didn't stop us from driving the two hours to see each other. And when we couldn't do that, we'd talk on the phone for hours on end. I was falling for him.

One day when Nick drove down to see Alison, before he visited her, he came to see me. We went to the park. We were walking when he suddenly stopped, took my hands in his and told me he thought he was falling in love with me. I was stunned. But happy, too. He told me that since the first day he met me he thought I was special. He said it hurt him to think another boy could like me as much as he did me. Hearing his words is what I had been waiting for: to have a boy feel this way about me and tell me these beautiful words. He said it was difficult to "live a lie" but next to impossible to ignore his feelings for me. I told him I felt the same way about him, that he was the guy I saw when I closed my eyes. That he was the guy I wanted to take me to the winter ball. I was about to tell him a million more things, but before I could say another word, he kissed me.

So that was how things started. Nick and Alison then broke up. For the next month Nick drove to visit me every week. Week by week, our relationship grew. It was awesome. But then Nick didn't show up in the place we'd always met—the coffeehouse. I sat in the coffee shop for three hours waiting for him, but he never showed. I went home. There was a message waiting for me from Nick asking me to call him.

I called him. He apologized for keeping me waiting in the coffee shop and then told me that on the way to meet me, he'd run into Alison. They had talked and were now back together. He said he was sorry that we couldn't continue to see each other. He decided he still wanted to see Alison. He said he was driving over on Saturday, and he wanted to tell me in person.

So here I stood, my heart crying: the guy I liked made a choice—and it wasn't me! How do you find fault with someone saying, "I've got to follow my heart"?

If it took courage for him to follow the orders of his heart, then I'd have to tell my heart to "march on" as well. March on out of his life. Hurt and devastated, but having heard the pain in his voice, all I could do was say, "I understand." Too stunned to cry, and too brave to get mad at him, I gathered my courage and sweetly said "I'll never forget you."

"I know," was all he said.

As hurt as I was, I knew how difficult it was for him to tell me, and how much courage it took to tell me in person. I think it takes real courage to end a relationship with someone you love. And courage to end things peacefully. And courage to go on. And courage to believe that one day I will find love again.

—Elizabeth Moria, 17

Movie Star; Math Genius

Sometimes it takes someone else believing in you before you can believe in yourself.
—**Danica McKellar, 29**

I had always been an A student, and I was starting junior high with expectations. But I had enrolled in the honors math class and found myself struggling just to keep up. I had always done well in math in elementary school; why was this so different? Things got progressively worse; I couldn't understand a thing our teacher was telling us! I remember wrestling with homework assignments for hours on end, and my grades were slowly but surely sliding downward.

Midway through the year, the school switched our teacher and we were given Mrs. Jacobson to finish out the course. She was friendly and helpful, but at that point I was convinced that I simply would never understand math. Things continued to get worse for me—it looked like I might fail the class.

And then came the day for the dreaded quiz. Mrs. Jacobson had handed out the quiz, and as I sat there reading it, I could have sworn it was written in some other language. I had NO IDEA how to proceed. The page remained blank for the entire time, and the only thoughts going through my head were, "I can't do this!" and "I don't belong here!"

The recess bell rang, and my page was still blank. I remember holding back the tears, trying so hard not to cry. Other students all stood up and turned in their quizzes. I just couldn't move. How could I turn in a blank test?

After everyone else had left, Mrs. Jacobson walked over to me and said, "Why don't you keep working on the quiz through recess?" I stared up at her through my watery gaze, and she just nodded at me and sat down at her desk. What did this mean?

She wanted me to work on the quiz during recess. She would do that for me. Grateful and energized, I got to work on the math problems in front of me. Inspired by the opportunity for a second chance, my brain started to function. Suddenly some of the questions began to make some sense. I was finding some success with it! When recess was over, I handed the quiz back to her and went on to my next class. We never spoke about it again.

I got a C on that quiz—75 percent. Somehow in that fifteen minutes of recess, I managed to get 75 percent of the answers correct! How had it happened? Why did she do that for me, and why was I suddenly able to think clearly? As my grades in that class quickly began to improve, and I finished out the year with an A, I finally realized something: The teacher gave me the extra time that day because she believed in me—when I couldn't believe in myself. It made all the difference.

I recently graduated UCLA summa cum laude with a degree in mathematics, where I also tutored calculus for two years. Since then, I've spoken to Congress on the importance of women in mathematics. I am now a published mathematician, after coauthoring a new theorem. I am also a spokesperson for a middle-school math organization called Figure This!, which helps middle-school students with math. I also answer math questions on my Web site. Today, although I now work primarily as an actress, my hobby of mathematics continues to be a source of joy and intellectual thriving. And I love sharing my passion for math with others.

I don't know if this all would've happened if not for Mrs. Jacobson, but I do know that in that moment when she had a little faith in me, I believed that I was worth that faith. That really grew my courage. From this experience I learned that sometimes it takes someone else believing in you before you can believe in yourself. Just as Mrs. Jacobson was there for me, I can be there for you, too. Math really can be a fun subject, and I encourage all of you to face it without fear.

—**Danica McKellar, 29**
actress from television's The Wonder Years and
The West Wing

"No Plea Bargains"

I've learned that justice may be hard to accept when it lands on us personally, but it's fair, and it's impartial. So now, I think about the consequences of my actions—beforehand!

—Danny Morse, 16

I sat waiting for the principal to see me, scared as only a thirteen-year-old who knows he's in some serious trouble can be. I only came to the office because I believed I'd be caught sooner or later, and I figured things would go better for me if I confessed instead of waiting to be caught. It seemed like a good idea just a few hours ago. Now, sitting here thinking things over, I wondered just how to explain it so that Mr. Camp would understand—and give me a break.

What happened was this: On Saturday night I'd been invited to spend the night at Shane's house. He's my best friend. I got there as planned, around six o'clock. We started out watching Star Wars and then played video games. Around nine o'clock we decided it would be fun to set up his tent and camp out in the backyard. We'd just hauled the tent into the backyard when Shane's older brother, Drake, came home from an evening out with his friends. He asked what we were doing, we told him, and he said he'd help us. The three of us put up the tent and then carried out sleeping bags, pillows, a flashlight, sodas, a boom box, popcorn and chips. You would have thought we were going to camp out for a week! About an hour into our "camp out," we got tired of eating and listening to music and went back into the house to hang out with Drake, who was watching television in the family room. When he asked us why we were in the house, we told him we were bored and were trying to think of something fun to do. Drake suggested all three of us take a walk over to our school grounds. So off we went.

It was almost 10:30 when we arrived at Potter Junior High. "Let's see if we can get in," Drake said, checking to see if any of the lower windows would open. The third one he tried was unlocked. Drake gave Shane a leg up through the open window, and then me. Shane somehow made it up on his own. We all fell into a pile on the floor of the classroom inside, laughing, partly at our own pileup and partly to hide our nervousness. The room looked weird in the dark, especially since the security lights outside cast just enough light to make out the chairs and desks in the room. "This is Miss Murray's room," I said. "She's my English teacher."

"Geez, I hate that woman," Shane remarked. The next thing I knew, we were emptying the contents of her desk drawers all over the floor. We ripped down the papers and posters from the bulletin boards, pulled books off the shelves and kicked the desks all over the room. Egging each other on only made us want to do more. "Let's do old Foley's room,"

Drake suggested. "I used to give him so much crap! I can't believe he's still here. Well, I can. He'll teach until the day he dies!" We were off, and when we had trashed it, we hit my "most-hated" teacher, Mrs. Henderson. Minutes later we were scrambling up and out the window we'd entered. Our adrenaline pumping, we ran the entire way home. Once home, you would have thought we'd talk and laugh about things, but we were all quiet.

As morning dawned, I laid awake back in the tent—already worried. What's going to happen if I'm caught? Somebody could have seen us! I wonder if they'll do fingerprints! What if there was a security camera! Why did I do something so stupid—what was I thinking? The next three days and three nights were the most miserable of my life. I couldn't sleep and whenever a teacher looked at me in class, I was sure that teacher knew I'd been a part of the destruction—or maybe even that I'd done it all. By Wednesday I was such a wreck I thought it would be a relief to confess. So here I sat waiting for Mr. Camp. Just then he opened his door. "You want to see me, Danny?" he asked, looking friendly and concerned. Not really, I thought, knowing the friendly look would be wiped away in moments. But it was too late to turn back. "Yes," I said, taking a deep breath and rising slowly to my feet. "What's up?" he asked, taking his chair and pointing for me to sit back down.

It took all the courage I had, but I blurted the

words I had rehearsed. "Mr. Camp, I was involved in the vandalism Saturday night." He sat back in his chair and just looked at me and then said, "Suppose you tell me what happened, from beginning to end." I launched into the story, trying my best to make it sound like a harmless prank gone awry. I ended my confession by assuring him, "We didn't have it planned. It just sorta happened."

"'Just sorta happened?'" Mr. Camp repeated. "Desks turned over. Drawers emptied. Property destroyed. And it 'just sorta happened'? I don't think so." He paused, obviously planning his move. "Well, Danny, the first thing I'm going to do is call your parents. Then I'm going to call the police. Your vandalism wasn't just a childish prank; it was a crime, a felony. They'll come and take you to the station, where you'll be booked. Eventually, you'll go see the judge. If you're lucky, he'll give you probation and hundreds of hours of community service. If you're not, you'll go to a juvenile detention center. What you've done is very serious."

My head was spinning. "But," I said, trying to defend myself, "I confessed. Doesn't that count for something? I admitted what I did and I'm sorry about it. Please don't call my parents. Why do you have to call the police?" I started to cry.

"Danny," Mr. Camp responded. "I am very encouraged that you came to me and confessed. That took a lot of guts, and I respect you for that. However, you must realize that your confession in no way diminishes the wrong you've done. There are consequences to wrong behavior, and you need to learn that now."

"But when criminals confess, they get a lighter sentence," I pleaded. "Why shouldn't I?"

"That's known as a plea bargain," Mr. Camp explained. "It happens when a DA (district attorney) agrees to a lighter sentence in exchange for a confession or information. There are no plea bargains here." Confused and wishing I was anywhere but here turning myself in, I groaned, "But that's not fair."

"Let me explain 'fair,'" Mr. Camp said, folding his hands on his desk, leaning forward to meet my eyes more closely. "I care about you and believe that you are basically a good kid. I do not want to call your parents or the police. However, I'm going to because I am more interested in building your character than I am in making you feel like it's no big deal that you've done something gravely wrong. This is a basic truth: Our actions result in consequences. My calling your parents and the police isn't 'punishment' for the sake of revenge; it's a consequence of your bad choices. You've started to turn things around by making the right choice in confessing. Now let's see if you can face the penalty with the same integrity."

I sat stunned at the turn of events, crying as Mr. Camp made his phone calls—my stomach churning as I thought of all the trouble I'd made for myself. It was the worst day of my life, but, in a twisted way, it was also the best, because I learned something that will serve me for the rest of my life: Justice may be hard to accept when it lands on us personally, but it's fair, and it's impartial. Mr. Camp was right. Justice is the line between right and wrong, and when we learn that, it can help us choose which side of the line we want to be on. I kept reminding myself of that as I faced my parents and appeared before the judge and did my thousands of hours of community service and worked to repay my one-third of the damage we three had done.

That was three years ago; the time it took me to complete my service hours, after which my record was cleared. It's over and done with now. Though I wouldn't recommend learning the hard way, as I did, I do know that we are free to choose if we'll just follow the crowd—or do our own thinking. As for me, I now have more than enough courage to do my own thinking, always considering the consequences of my actions—beforehand!

—Danny Morse, 16

Summer Love

When Chris asked me out, I was overjoyed. I didn't think he saw me as anything more than a friend. I was crazy about him.

I was mesmerized, just totally entranced by him:

- So, what if I could hardly get a word in edgewise?
- So, what if I always measured my words, making sure I didn't say anything that might upset him because then he'd sulk for the rest of the evening?
- So, what if he didn't seem all that interested in my opinions?
- So, what if, depending on his always changing moods, he would be nice to me one minute, and then short and impatient the next?
- So, what if when we were with friends he mostly ignored me?
- So, what if he often was late in picking me up?
- So, what if he wasn't sensitive to the fact that I didn't care for the food at the fast-food stand where we often ate?
- So, what if I spent hours getting ready but he seemed to never notice? I always wanted to tell him how I felt about this treatment but didn't.

We dated all that summer. But when school started, he dumped me, and found someone else. Don't you just hate it when you discover that all the reasons for not being with someone were there all along and you just chose to ignore them?

—Katie Ionata, 17

The "Lauren Club"

So many times, I'd sit in class worrying about who did or didn't like me. I don't go there anymore. I now haver the courage to remain true to myself, refusing to buy into any of the cliques at school, and still be liked.

—Lauren Gay, 14

When I was in elementary school I had a very close group of friends. We had been together for six years, kindergarten through fifth grade (some of us had even gone to preschool together). We were all in the same classes together year after year. We played games and sports together. We went on skiing and snowboarding trips to neat new places (even out of state!) like Colorado and Idaho. We went backpacking and on fishing trips. We went on church retreats. Everybody was invited to everyone's birthday parties. We helped each other do homework. We stood up for each other. Our parents carpooled. We were more like a family than just classmates. For sure, most all of us considered ourselves to be each other's friends.

Then came middle school. I didn't expect things to change, but they did. Within weeks different kids began forming cliques. My old friends and I were no different. We formed one, too. I wasn't all that surprised that we were the coolest because we were: We were smart and funny, very social, had quick wits, dressed nice and listened to the latest music. We emerged as the "most popular" group. As for the girls in the group, we were the girls other that girls wanted to be like.

I enjoyed being part of this group; it was great. At least in the beginning. It wasn't long before this group, my old friends, began to change. One day two of my old friends, two of the "most popular" girls, walked up to another kid and began saying sarcastic things to him, calling him "a nerd" and "a loser." They called him other things, too, nasty things that I can't put in writing. I was shocked they were so mean to someone. It really made me uncomfortable, and I was embarrassed. It got worse. Within no time, this sort of thing began to happen a lot. Pretty soon it became a normal thing that happened all the time. Suddenly, in our group name-calling, cruelty and profanity were "in." If you weren't in the group, not only were you "not cool," but you were fair game for these attacks. I was sure it must have been awful to be confronted by members of our group. We weren't all that great to each other, either. We got so used to dumping on other kids that we started doing it to each other, too, sometimes even when outsiders were around. I was really feeling stressed out: I knew the way our group was treating other kids, and even ourselves, wasn't right. And yet, I didn't want to give up the benefits and status I had because I was part of this group. It felt nice to be envied and thought of as the "best" or "coolest." I know that sounds terrible, but I'd be lying if I didn't admit that it was true.

Then, fate sort of just stepped in. As it turned out, I didn't have many classes with my old group of friends and so I was meeting a lot of new kids, and a lot of us were becoming friends. Little by little I began spending more time with this new group, a group that was pretty much thought of as a "class act." Like the "most popular" group, they were smart, had fun parties, wore neat clothes, listened to popular music and were good athletes. They had everything going for them my old friends did, except they were nicer. They didn't get their kicks by making other kids feel bad so that they could feel better or more important. Best of all, they were hardly ever mean to anyone.

What a relief. It was such a big change from the "most popular" group. And a good feeling. I liked being with them because it felt like the old days when everyone supported each other. How different this was from my old friends. They always had a new rumor to spread, always a new victim to harass, always a teacher they were out to get. For all the benefits I got from being part of the "most popular" group, as exciting as it was and as flattering as it was, and for all the "bonding" with the coolest kids it produced, it was also stressful, tiring and time-consuming. And, of course, to make things worse, I knew a lot of what we were doing was not only mean, it was wrong. At the time though, I didn't have the courage to do anything but to look after myself.

So here I am, one foot in the "most popular" clique, and one foot in the "class act" group but needing (and wanting) to choose to belong to either one or the other. While stressing out over it, I tried to understand why some kids, like my old friends, were more popular than others. They didn't dress any differently, weren't any prettier, smarter or better athletes. So why did other girls, including some of my new friends, envy my old friends, and want to be like them and accepted by them? Then it came to me. The "most popular" were most popular because they acted and advertised that they were! They just put it "out there" that they were the most popular, and so other kids thought so, too. It was that simple.

I learned something else: Cliques demand total loyalty and commitment, as well as conformity. While the members choose who can join, initially, the group then makes you choose to be "in" or "out." Not that they must pressure you a whole lot to make a choice. It's difficult, if not impossible, to "belong" to two (or more) groups at the same time. Each group is always doing different things, in different places, at the same time, and going to different parties at the same time. Who can be in two or more places at the same time? I couldn't. But even before the "most popular" group could force me to choose, my new friends, the "class act" club talked to me about it. Even my new friends thought I had to make a choice. How, they said, could I be doing things with them and with my old friends at the same time? They weren't mean about it; they just wanted to see me more often.

But it wasn't easy to pick one friend or friends over another. Yes, I really admired my new friends, the "class act" kids, but I'd spent practically my entire life with my old friends, who were still my friends even though I knew they weren't perfect, and besides, I had to admit, I liked being seen as one of the "most popular." Talk about stress! I was forced to really think things through. The two groups, my old friends, and my new ones, were alike in a lot of ways, but they were different in the way they treated people. One was mean and exclusive, the other friendly and supportive.

But I knew I didn't want to be mean to other kids, and I didn't want them to be mean to me. I started leaning toward choosing my new friends over my old ones. I began by mostly hanging out more with my new friends. Still, a couple times a week I would spend time with my old friends, like have lunch with them, see them at church or play sports with them. It was hard giving them up as close friends, even though they were mean sometimes, because they could also be a lot of fun to be with and they did a lot of fun things. Still, being part of both groups was confusing, to me and to them. No one, including myself, knew where I belonged, and you were supposed to know where you belonged—everyone was supposed to know where you belonged.

I began to think that maybe it wasn't impossible to belong to two groups at once. We had been able to have a lot of different friends before we got to middle school. Why couldn't we do it again? Maybe I could make it work. What if I refused to join either group? What if I remained true to myself, and what I thought was right, refusing to buy into "membership" at all? Could I be myself, be with all sorts of kids, and still be liked and accepted? Would the "Lauren Club of One" mean that I'd be left out and home alone or could I be the "Lauren Club of One and Many," the one being me and the many being both my old friends and my new ones. A lot of kids thought I was crazy, and I was confused and unsure, but I decided to take a chance and to find out. I did.

I couldn't believe what happened. I hoped it would work out, but honestly had my doubts! I thought I would end up the "Lauren Club of One" with no friends. But the "Lauren Club of One and Many" is working out, and it has been accepted! It's great. My old friends and I still get to do a lot of things together, as do my new friends and me. And because I'm seen as me and not just as a member of a group where everyone is pretty much viewed as being the same, I get to be myself. I've really learned a lot.

Looking back at all the time I spent sitting in class wondering and worrying about who would like me and who wouldn't, now I don't go there anymore. I'm not saying I still don't face challenge and uncertainty, or that maybe things will change, and I'll get a different lesson in friendship and membership in cliques a week or a month or a year from now. I'm just saying that I'm happy I found the courage to stay with my decision. I'm no longer totally stressed. Now I can hang with my newer friends at school and do stuff with them, but I still see my old friends around and we still do stuff together, too.

The courage to be true to yourself can be a good thing.

—**Lauren Gay, 15**

Courage Can Enlightened Your Perspective

I think everyday takes courage.
                              —**Brooke L. Kuiper, 15**

I've learned that blinkers are important.

I've learned that someone can love you a lot and not know how to show it.

I've learned that you can make someone's day by simply smiling.

I've learned that singing "Amazing Grace" can lift my spirits.

I've learned that you can tell a lot about someone by the size of a tip he or she leaves at the restaurant.

I've learned that regardless of how much you argue with your parents, you miss them when you're on a trip.

I've learned that supermodels are not always as the girl sitting next to you in class.

I've learned not to pet porcupines.

I've learned that some questions ("Does this pimple look terrible?") should not be answered.

I've learned crying can make you feel better.

I've learned everyone comes into your life for a reason.

I've learned that not all locks are meant to be opened.

I've learned to forgive myself for not being born a genius.

I've learned there is no Santa Claus or Easter Bunny, and that my mother is not the Tooth Fairy.

I've learned that my parents sometimes lie to protect me from the pain of the truth.

I've learned that when the door says "push," I shouldn't pull.

I've learned that most pickup lines backfire.

I've learned that junior high and high school relationships are not forever.

I've learned that you shouldn't tailgate.

I've learned that when you speed over bumps,

you can count on biting your tongue.

I've learned that police officers have little or no sense of humor.

I've learned that it's best to keep thinking about the words you say because tomorrow you may have to eat them.

I've learned that college is not for everyone.

I've learned that sometimes success is just making it through the day.

I've learned that light sockets are not made for paper clips.

I've learned dog kisses can make anything better.

I've learned parents make mistakes, too.

I've learned that just because you hide your vegetables at the table doesn't mean they're gone for good.

I've learned teachers don't always have the right answers.

I've learned it's better to be slow and careful than fast and careless.

I've learned lima beans are never delicious.

I've learned that not all love is forever.

I've learned that looking back on tears can make you laugh.

I've learned that sometimes "I'm sorry" just doesn't cut it.

I've learned sometimes the nerdy guy DOES get the girl.

I've learned that tomorrow will always remember what you put off doing today.

I've learned to worry less about what I have and concentrate on giving more.

I've learned that a bad experience can be a blessing in disguise.

I've learned to use my mistakes to my advantage.

I've learned being popular means you don't have to live by the same set of rules as everyone else.

I've learned that having a crush on someone can make you crazy.

I've learned that no matter how old you are,

body noises are funny.

I've learned a person can be ignorant but not stupid. On the other hand, a person can be intelligent and not smart.

I've learned that being book smart does not mean you have common sense.

I've learned manners can take you a long way.

I've learned to pay attention to the doors that have been opened for you.

I've learned that in the scheme of things, the little things really don't matter; it's the little things that can make your life miserable.

I've learned if you are going to dish it out, you better be able to take it.

I've learned that my dog doesn't like to wear sunglasses.

I've learned that cement is unforgiving.

I've learned that the "Matrix" is not real.

I've learned that a car accident can break my bones.

I've learned that traffic signs are not merely suggestions.

I've learned that bicycles are not bigger than cars.

I've learned that even when a boy/girlfriend kisses your bruise, it still hurts.

I've learned that some secrets are not meant to be told.

I've learned that 911 is for extreme emergencies only.

I've learned not to do things behind my parents' back.

I've learned never to embarrass anyone in public.

I've learned that a roll of toilet paper won't flush.

I've learned that just because someone smiles, it doesn't mean that he or she is happy.

I've learned that dressing up makes me feel better.

I've learned that playing hooky means you're going to end up in trouble.

I've learned that you should never jump into water when you can see the bottom.

I've learned that I like people when they sing the national anthem.

I've learned that our dog doesn't want to eat my broccoli, either.

I've learned that when I wave to people, they wave back.

I've learned that if you want to cheer yourself up, cheer someone else up.

I've learned that life sometimes gives you a second chance.

I learned I can count on myself to mostly make the right decision.

I've learned that everyone likes it when you say, "I'll keep you in my prayers."

I've learned that it pays to believe in miracles.

I've learned that people love a friendly pat on the back.

I've learned that I still have a lot to learn.

I've learned that being kind is more important than being right.

I've learned that sometimes all a person needs is a hand to hold and a heart to understand.

I've learned that when I'm upset with Mom or Dad, a walk around the block is all it takes to understand where they are "coming from."

I've learned that under everyone's "tough kid" act is secret pain that hurts a lot.

I've learned that to ignore the facts does not change the facts.

I've learned that you shouldn't ignore the dragon if you live next to a dragon farm.

I've learned that when you plan to get even with someone, you are only letting that person continue to hurt you more.

I've learned that I can't choose how I feel, but I can choose what I do about it.

I've learned that a smile is a great way to improve your looks.

I've learned that being nice to others not only brightens up their day but sweetens mine, as well.

I've learned that I am a very courageous person.
—Brook L. Kuiper, 15

"Not Even a Star Can Outdo the Moon!"

When you lose someone, you revisit your last moments together and play them over and repeatedly. It makes me realize how important it is that all our moments be kind and loving toward each other.

—Mandy Martinez, 18

One evening several years ago Mom and I were watching an episode of The Wonder Years. "Life spins like a dime and cuts like a knife," someone on the show remarked. "What's that mean, Mom?" I asked. "It means life goes by quickly and hurts when it's over," she replied, matter-of-factly. "Oh," I said, dismissing it because I couldn't relate. Today I can relate. I know exactly what the phrase means. I've just lost my mother in a car crash, and the pain is so deep it cuts to the bone.

It's only been months since my mother died, but already it feels like she's been gone a lifetime. There are days I think I can't make it through. We were so close, and we loved each other so much. The hole in my heart is bigger than the planet. And everything that happens is a gigantic reminder of just how tragic the loss is. Mom died three days before my eighteenth birthday and only a week before my older brother Robert's birthday. Two months after Mom died, my sister got married—without her own mother to see her on this momentous day. My sister also celebrated her birthday recently—without our mother. My little brother, Dylan, entered his freshman year without his mother and played his first varsity football game without his mother in the stands to proudly watch her freshman son play on a varsity team! Dylan, too, just recently celebrated a birthday—his fifteenth—without his mother. My older brother had his twenty-sixth birthday without her. She missed my first and only prom. And I graduated from high school without her cheering me on, without her ever seeing me reach this great accomplishment, something that was so important to her.

Graduation was especially tough without her. I wore a button with her picture on it so that I could feel she was there with me. I remember standing on stage waiting for my name to be called so I could come forward and get my diploma. The moment I did, I instinctively investigated the audience, searching for her face. Getting a grip on the fact that she wouldn't be there, of course, I soothed myself by saying over and over, "Good job, Moon!" "Good job, Moon!"—which is exactly what she would have told me—a thousand times!—that day. I touched her button before walking across and I thought, She's proud, she's proud. She would have been soooooo proud.

Every family member tried to make up for the loss of her not being there. My sister had given me a handbag and a charm with a heart that had a cross inside. She also wrote me a nice letter, saying how sorry she was Mom couldn't be there to see this, but how I should believe Mom was there watching it all, anyway. The charm had been her last Christmas gift from Mom. She wanted me to wear it as I took my walk across the graduation stage that day. In fact, I was wearing three things pinned to me that day! All held memories of life and times with a young mother we dearly loved.

Memories. So many memories. What I've discovered is that when you lose someone, you revisit your last moments together and play them over and over. In my case, Mom had just picked me up from school. We'd stopped for food, and then she'd said, "I've got to go pick up your brother. Want to come along or be dropped at home?"

"I want to go home," I told her. "I'd like to go get online." "Okay," she said, cheerfully. We took things into the house from the car. Turning to leave, she said, "Lock the door, Moon." (My mother was fond of telling the story that as a baby, my eyes were as big as a full moon. Then, because my baby brother pronounced my name [Mandy] as "Moondee," the nickname Moon stuck.)

"As if a robber is going to come out and get me!" I replied, laughing. Mom laughed at that comeback. And in the next moment, our baby kitten, seeing the open door, decided to seize an opportunity to sneak outside. The mother cat lay nearby and lazily opened only one eye, watching her wild and bratty little kitten lower his head and belly to the floor (perhaps thinking he then wouldn't be seen), and then, like a bolt of lightning, streak to the door in an attempt to escape. It was a cute and sinister moment from the little creature, and Mom and I caught it. Instinctively, we looked at each other and then broke out laughing. Mom hurriedly pushed the door shut and said, "Look at her watch her kitten! She knew the little creep wouldn't make it past us! She's probably busting up inside laughing!" Again, we laughed together. "Well, lock up then, honey. I'll be right back, Moon. Love you," she said. "Love you," I told her. I waved good-bye. Those were our last moments together. It was to be the last time I'd see my mother alive. Five minutes later, she was dead.

I loved her laugh. I miss it so much. I am so happy our last moments were those in which we were so happy, laughing and most of all, moments in which we told each other of our love for each other. It makes me realize how important it is that all our moments be kind and loving toward each other.

Those first moments I learned of her death were insane. I didn't know what to do with myself. My mother was dead (she was only forty-six)! I was inconsolable. I cried and screamed because the rage I felt for her loss was larger than the air around me. I yelled and screamed at God for taking her, and at the same time begged Him to soothe the searing ache in my heart. I walked to the kitchen, where

Mom had set down the remains of the fast food we had stopped to get. I remember putting my hand inside the bag to touch the hamburgers—still warm. I touched her raspberry drink—still cold. I thought, *the hamburgers haven't even gotten cold; her drink hasn't become room temperature, but she had time enough to lose her life. It can't be possible.*

Mom was killed turning onto the highway, a path she'd taken day after day, year after year. But as fate would have it, this would be her last time to ever make that turn. She was hit by an eighteen-wheel truck that had crossed into her lane. She must have been so terrified to see death coming upon her like that.

Her life was over. Our lives together were over.

The viewing, one day after my eighteenth birthday, was filled with stark moments. They were especially painful for me because this was my mother. But they were awful because I felt the pain and anguish of my little brother facing this terrible reality as well. I found myself unable to walk up to see her without my little brother by my side. My little brother didn't want to either. "I won't go if you don't," I told him. As though we each were doing it for the other, the two of us managed to make it to the side of our mother's casket. She looked asleep in the casket. Seeing Mom, little Dylan stood there and repeated, "That's not Momma. That's not my momma." He was dazed as was I. All I could say was, "Her neck hurts when she sleeps like that." Lost in grief, I was totally disoriented. I just looked at her and thought, she just bruised her face, she's fine. But of course, she wouldn't be "just fine"; in the accident, her neck had been broken, causing her death.

Dylan and I put our hands on her shoulder. "She's cold," my little brother said, patting her forehead. I didn't want to touch her: Reality then might become real, and I wasn't ready to accept it. I had brought a couple of things with me I wanted to place in her casket. I had brought my drawing of a picture of Jesus, a picture of us kids, and a "Mother" plaque I bought her just a few short weeks ago.

Finally, I kissed the top of her head, but only at the hairline. Not too close to her forehead because I didn't want to feel that she might be cold. I kissed her and whispered, "Good night, Mom." I didn't plan on saying anything at all. It just came out. It was as if my own mind was in the ozone somewhere. I kept thinking of all the times I'd come home late from being with my friends, and there she was, sitting in her recliner waiting up for me. I so wanted to go back to that place. I looked at the flowers surrounding the casket, and then became aware of everyone crying.

I broke down then, too. The pain was just so awful.

Her memorial service was two days later, three days after my eighteenth birthday. My aunt was one of the people who stood up and talked. She told people how my mom was—in a very real way, a mother to her, too. Then it was my turn to say something, and I started to cry before I even spoke. I wanted what I was going to say to be clear. But it wasn't. "I'm going to read a poem I read to Mom on our trip to Missouri," I told everyone. "She told me when she died, she wanted me to read it. I'm going to read this." I looked out to everyone and they were all a blur. I began reading what I considered my mother's poem, which is really a well-known poem called "A Clown's Prayer." "Dear Lord," I began. "As I stumble through this life, help me to create more laughter than tears, dispense more happiness than gloom, spread more cheer than despair. Never let me become so blasé that I fail to see the wonder in the eyes of a child, or a twinkle in the eyes of the aged. Never let me forget my work is to cheer people, make them happy, and make them laugh. Make them forget at least for a moment the unpleasantness in their life. Never let me acquire success to the point that I discontinue calling on my creator in the hour of need, acknowledging and thanking Him in the hour of plenty. And in my final moment may I hear You whisper, 'When you made My people smile, you made me smile.'"

It was difficult to get through because I was crying so hard. I remember looking out into the crowd at the many who had gathered to send my mother off to heaven, and telling them how I felt she was, somehow, still here with us. Everything from that point on is pretty much a blur. Like her life, the memorial service was over all too quickly.

In all, I believe we've lost more than just a mother. We lost a friend, a sister and a daughter—and more. She was the miracle of inspiration for all we hoped to achieve; there was such joy and happiness in her eyes. "I can't wait to tell Mom" was a line a heard a million times from all of us. She was a positive and strong-willed person who would go the distance for you—and she always supported you in going the distance.

My dream was to have her watch me walk across the stage and get my high school diploma. I wanted her to see all that I was to make of life in the future. My little brother's dream was to have her there to watch him play on the "Big Boy's Field" (that's what she called it) for his freshman football games. My sister's dream was to have her be there for her wedding. My older brother's dream was to buy her new glasses for her birthday. All those dreams are history now. Sometimes I make a list of things she's going to miss, so that I can deal with them and get them out of the way. There are, of course, a lot of things I still must deal with because they're not going to go away soon—like having to drive on the road and the very spot where she was killed. Never do I cross that place without my heart skipping a beat.

Just as my life is different now, I am different now.

I once considered my life as rather typical. Each

day came and went. Overall, I was a girl who lived inside my own little world, a world where life inside my imagination was bigger and better than what happened. Friends, school life and boys were everything. It was "all about me." But no more. I no longer have the luxury of living life slowly or on a small scale. My mother's death has caused me to stand straight and square my shoulders to the world. I am no longer a girl now. I am a woman. It's time for me to take my mother's place in giving all the love and good she sent into the world.

Once focused on my own little world, I'm now focused on a bigger picture. Once insecure and worried about "little" things, I have no more time for that. It is time for me to step forward and be more. I must "outdo the moon" now. I remember back to all those times when I did feel insecure or unsure of myself, and Mom would playfully cajole: "Oh, you can do it! Believe in yourself, honey! Not even a star can outdo my Moon!" To remember these playful words and especially to not hear her say them breaks my heart. To have lost that kind of love and support is a scary feeling. Still, I must go on now. I must believe her words; I must LIVE her words. And so, I can and will do it.

In a sense, I'm writing this story now for her. I told Mom I wanted to write a story and send it in to see if I could get published. My mother was thrilled that I was doing something "so grand," as she described it. The story did not get published, but the authors wrote me back and encouraged me to rewrite it and try again. My mother picked right up on this and encouraged me. Excited, I rewrote my story, "Ciara's Music Box," reading it to my mother a hundred-and-one times. When my mother gave a thumbs-up, I sent it in. Sure enough, the story was accepted.

That I'd been published was thrilling. But it was my mother's reaction that made it more exciting. She was so celebratory over it! When word came that my story had made it in the book, we sang and laughed and danced around the room! She could be so crazy—she was so young at heart. I loved that about her. "Stars can NOT even outdo my Moon!" she said, laughing and proud of the fact her daughter had a story accepted for publication. And then, "Do it again, Moon!" she encouraged, "Do it again."

I will. Not only because it will make my mother proud, but because my heart goes out to any young person who has suffered a loss as great as mine and can take comfort in knowing that giving words to your grief helps—at least a little. And I must also do it because life is short—and I don't want to miss a day of it. I never thought losing anyone would be this hard. But life has given me my reality check; I must "cash" it. I just find a way to go on.

If you are so lucky as to have your mom or dad alive, be so thankful. Don't wait for a reason to tell them you appreciate and love them. Show it in all you say and do. Because if one day you should, like me, get that phone call that will change your life forever, you just don't want to regret that you didn't. And with that said, I have words for you, too, Mother. I know you know this, but it helps for me to say it. "I'll never give up; I will strive to be all you wished me to be. I'll try my best to become the awesome and loving woman you are. I'll look out for my little brother, so don't worry about him. And I'll do all I can to see that we kids always love and look out for each other. Thank you for loving me so much, and for being the sort of person who is worthy of the enormously searing hurt I now feel. But I'll see you again, Mom. I know it for real. Love, your Moon."

—Mandy "Moon" Martinez, 18

My Turn Up to Bat

Part of how I'm healing the hurt of my father's death is through achievement—through setting goals and accomplishing them.
—Thomas L. Watson Jr., 18

My dad was killed, along with his copilot, in a small-plane crash. My dad was piloting the plane. While taxiing down the runaway, the plane hit a patch of sand and skidded out of control, crashing into another plane.

I won't ever forget that day, though I have put much of the grieving behind me. My biggest goal now is to be focused. I want my father to be proud of me. And I want others to see and know me, and to think that my dad must have been a great father to raise someone as strong and successful as me.

My dad was a great man. He was a good father and a good husband. He was an attorney with a very successful practice. I carry his name: Thomas L. Watson Jr. For that, I am proud and thankful. This is another reason that I want to fulfill his legacy. I don't feel that I am forgoing my life in completing his. Being an attorney is something I genuinely want to do, but reaching the goal is especially important since it was something my father was excited about as well. He and I often talked about how the sign on our office would be Watson & Watson—Attorneys at Law. Always, I told him that I wasn't sure if I was smart enough to make it through so much school. "You can do it, son," he'd always say to me. "The most important part is making the decision to pick up the bat and step up to the plate. After that, it's all pretty easy."

I miss him so much, but it is exactly at those times that I remind myself to "pick up the bat and step up to the plate." Especially when I'm hurting or missing Dad, I try to make sure that I'm on track with my plans. Not that I'm overlooking taking the time to grieve his death. But a good part of how I'm healing the hurt of my father's death is through achievement—through setting goals and accomplishing them. All this will help make the future happen. For example, getting into a good college is important. I'm going to have to pay for college myself, so I'm a serious student because I need decent grades to win a scholarship. But knowing what I'm aiming for at least makes me work for grades without complaining. I go the extra mile because it's important that I do.

Mom is a big help, too. I'm good with her, and I try not to cause her to worry about me. She says to me, "You're so like your father. You even have his values." I love it when she says that. And I think she's right. My dad and mom were really in love, so I want to be married someday. I'd like to be married to someone as loving and kind as my mother. I want to have the kind of supportive marriage the two of them had. I have one sister, and I think Mom and Dad would have had more kids.

Mom says they wanted more. I want kids, and I want to marry someone with family values. I really can't talk about these things with others my age because these sorts of goals seem so "grown-up" to many my age. And why not; they would be to me, too, if it weren't for the fact that having lost my dad means that I've had to grow up faster. But I'm okay with that, too. I feel a little alone, but I stay focused. Dad would want that. I want that. I want to become as much like my father as I can.

I'd say that my father has had a good influence on me. For sure, his death has shaped my goals, or in the least, caused me to feel that, yes, I can "pick up the bat and step up to the plate." As a result, I hope to have the courage to carry on the legacy of being a great guy just like my father.

—Thomas L. Watson Jr., 18

"And the Grammy for Best New Group Goes to . . ."

Have big dreams... You'll grow into them.
—Anonymous

When I gathered a couple of buddies to start a band, in the beginning we were just awful. But that's to be expected. We were just learning to play, and our singing, well, let's just say we were rough and off-key. So as not to scare the people and pets in the neighborhood, we hung carpet on the walls of the garage as a sound barrier. Disorganized was our middle name, though in those early days, it would have been a good name for our band as well. When we got tired of practicing—or couldn't take anymore, whichever came first—we'd walk out, leaving guitars, drums and drumsticks scattered everywhere. We knew "good" and "a shot at the big time" were awhile off! We now look back with laughter.

But even with others criticizing us and not believing in what we were doing, we kept to our music. Always we reminded ourselves of the goal: We were going to be musicians, outstanding ones. And we were going to write and record popular songs.

And yes, we were going to be famous. We stayed true to our goal even though in the early days of our band it was hard to get anyone to hire us, even if we agreed to play for free! Now we're getting good. We still meet people who do not believe in us, which brings this back to courage. In this business, while we get asked to play more and more, rejection is still high. But then again, we're going after some impressive billings these days. And with that, the possibility of rejection often gets larger. When it comes to courage, we know we need it. We've learned that others might not always believe in us, but we can always believe in ourselves.

I'm happy to report that we're finally at the stage where we've mastered our instruments, fine-tuned our voices and can admit that we're talented. I'm also pleased to report that now we're at the stage of looking to get a major label interested in us. We're hoping Sony will sign us, but there are three other good labels we're interested in as well. We have an agent, and we've recently cut a demo. When we heard it for the first time, we were thrilled.

I don't know if it will be a breakthrough for us, but we're hopeful. I'd say to you, have the courage to dream a big dream and head in that direction, no matter how many trials you must go through. I've found the courage to stay true to my goal. I'm not out to sell 120 albums. I'm out to sell 120 million albums.

I'm going to experience rejection. And success! I've got the courage to handle both!

—Beau Morris, 17

I am Terrified of Publicly Speaking...

I like to think of myself as courageous. I mean, I have no qualms about charging into the spotlight and dribbling through a zone press on the basketball court—everyone watching, and with "need to win this game" written on their faces.

I can hold my own when standing up to someone flirting with my girl or square off with a would-be bully just looking to pick a fight. But the thought of standing up in front of the entire class and making an oral report, now that is another matter!

I mean to tell you, before I even get to the front of the room, my heart starts beating and I swear it sounds as loud as thunder in a mountain storm.

Scared is not the worst of it. Always, I think, Oh, man, what if I get up there and can't remember what I'm supposed to say? I can see myself standing there, shaking, dry-mouthed, everyone staring at me in stone-cold silence while even my friends tried vainly to suppress their giggles. I sometimes actually wonder if a person could die from embarrassment. Sometimes I think I could! But I do know that I must overcome this fear—and the sooner the better, because if I don't it's going to follow me into college and maybe even when I go to work for some big company.

I know that if I don't learn to overcome this fear it will slow me down in life. After all, even corporate presidents give speeches to their board of directors and when appearing on camera for some charity or special event. What I most want to work on is developing the courage to speak in front of others.

—**Brad Tannen, 17**

Freedom Fighters Rank High on the Courage Scale

To me, those who serve in the many branches of the military—and freedom fighters everywhere—are brave and courageous beyond words.
—Hali Trask, 13

When I think of courage, for certain those who serve in the military come to mind. And for good reason! I have many family members who have been in the service—and some still are. My father, Dean Trask, was in the marine corps and served in Desert Storm (also known as the Gulf War). My great-grandfather, Everett Burres, served two terms in World War II, as did my other great-grandfather, Lawrence Derrig.

During the Vietnam War, my grandfather, Orval Kinne, was in the National Guard. During that same time, two great-uncles, Mark Burres and Kevin Burres, were in the service, too. I also have a step-great-grandfather, Charlie Wagner, who was in the Coast Guard. And Chaplain Jeff Struecker, who is my step-uncle, was also in the military and served in several war conflicts.

Having seen so many members of my family proudly serve their country, putting their lives on the line for our freedom, I have a real respect for them both as courageous people and as American soldiers. And because our family shares this legacy, I know from hearing their many conversations how courageous the many others who serve in the military are as well. To me, those who serve in the many branches of the military—and freedom fighters everywhere—are brave and courageous beyond words. Whether it's the marines, army, navy, air force, National Guard or Coast Guard, all who serve their country are heroes to me. All freedom fighters rank high on the courage scale in my book!

—Hali Trask, 13

CHAPTER 4

A Hero in the Making: My Personal Workbook

I Have to Live with Myself and So . . .

I have to live with myself and so,
I want to be fit for myself to know.
I want to be able as the days go by,
Always to look myself straight in the eye.
I don't want to stand with the setting sun,
And dislike myself for the things I've done.
I can never hide myself from me,
I see what others may never see.
I know what others may never know,
I can never fool myself and so . . .
Whatever happens I want to be,
Self-respecting and conscience free!
—Joy J. Golliver and Ruth Hayes-Arista
I CAN Ignite the Community Spirit

What does "I can never hide myself from me" mean to you?

_____

_____

_____

What does it mean to "always look myself straight in the eye"?

_____

_____

_____

BEING A PERSON OF INTEGRITY

Integrity is being right with yourself—no secrets, no dishonesty, just "what you see is what you get."

What does this quote mean to you?

_____

_____

What does having integrity mean to you?

_____

_____

Who of all the people you know—including your best friend, your mom or dad, brother or sister, or teachers—has the most integrity, and why?

_____

_____

Always do the right thing. This will gratify some people, and astonish the rest.

—Mark Twain

Do you think Mark Twain is right about the notion that doing the right thing will "astonish" some people? Why do you feel this way?

_____

_____

If someone doesn't agree with you, or doesn't think you did the right thing in a given situation, but you know in your heart that you did the right thing, what would you say to that person?

_____

_____

THE COURAGE TO DO THE RIGHT THING

I Lost a Fast Twenty Bucks

Several months ago while standing in the checkout line at the grocery store, I saw a twenty-dollar bill fall from a lady's purse as she took a check from her wallet. No one even noticed the money float to the floor. I was standing behind her waiting to pay for a bag of M&M's. I leaned over, tucked the cash into my hand and tightened my shoelaces. It was so tempting to pretend the only reason I'd bent down was to tie my shoes. I wanted to go to the fair with my friends on Saturday, and my parents had told me they weren't footing the bill, that I'd have to take care of it myself. I didn't have the money to go to the fair. I looked down at the bill in my hand, thinking that it sure would be handy to have that money! I thought about it—for about three seconds; I knew I had to give her the money back.

The woman was very grateful I found her money. I was grateful I had the courage to the right thing and give it back to her. I had taken the money, even though no one else might have found out, I would know. Then I'd have to think about how I had stolen it and live with feeling bad about doing it. Even if no one else finds out that you are an honest person, you know if you are or not.

I have integrity—with me.

—**Tomoko Ogata, 15**

What would you have done in Tomoko's situation? Why?

_____

_____

_____

Write about an incident where you were really tempted to be dishonest, but had the courage to do the right thing. What happened? Who was involved? How did things turn out?

_____

_____

How did doing the right thing make you feel about yourself?

_____

_____

Who, more than anyone else, instilled in you the value to do the right thing and why do you say this?

_____

_____

How does being able to count on yourself—to trust yourself— make you feel about yourself?

_____

_____

_____

KNOWING YOUR VALUES

List three values that are very important to you— and why each one is.

EXAMPLE:

<u>Value:</u> Keeping my word to my friends.

<u>Why this value is important to me:</u> It makes my friends trust me.

✓ Value: _____

Why this value is important to me:

_____

_____

✓ Value: _____

Why this value is important to me:

_____

_____

✓ Value: _____

Why this value is important to me:

_____

_____

If someone asked your best friend what you "stood for" (your values), would he or she mention the three you've listed?
❑ Yes   ❑ No

Do you and your friends share the same values? How can you tell?

_____

_____

How do you and your friends talk about what is right and wrong?

_____

_____

You gain strength, courage and confidence by every experience in which you really stop to look fear in the face.

—Eleanor Roosevelt

What does this quote mean to you?

_____

_____

_____

"The more of life I master, the less of life I fear."

—Eleanor Roosevelt

What does this quote mean to you?

_____

_____

_____

Describe a time when you faced a really big challenge and mastered it. What was the challenge? How did you "master" it?

_____

_____

_____

How did mastering that obstacle help you become a more confident and courageous person?

_____

_____

_____

The undertaking of a new action brings new strength.

—Evenius

What do you think this quote means?

_____

_____

_____

COURAGE AS A MUSCLE: SELF-DISCIPLINE

Self-discipline leads to convictions—which, in turn, contributes to a positive self-image, which, in turn, increases your self-esteem. It's a positive cycle helping you become a courageous person. Describe a time when that was true for you.

_____

_____

_____

Actions: Being Self-Disciplined

How does self-discipline lead to being courageous?

_____

_____

_____

Describe a time when you wanted to step forward, to take action, but didn't? What happened? Who was involved? How did things turn out? How did this make you feel about yourself?

_____

_____

_____

Whatever your past has been, you have a spotless future.

—Carushka

What does this quote mean to you?

_____

_____

_____

DECISIONS: BE A HERO

Everyone is somebody's hero!

—Anonymous

Do you agree with this quote? Do you think it's true that everyone is somebody's hero?

❑ Yes   ❑ No

What is a hero?

_____

_____

_____

Who's hero are you? How do you know that person thinks of you as his or her hero?

_____

_____

_____

Why does that person consider you his or her hero?

_____

_____

_____

Life shrinks or expands in proportion to one's courage.

—Anäis Nin

What does this quote mean to you?

_____

_____

Actions: Being a Hero

How do you define a hero? Who more than anyone else is your hero (or heroine)?

_____

_____

_____

Courage is not simply one the virtues, but the form of every virtue at the testing point.
—C.S. Lewis

What does this quote mean to you?

_____

_____

A person develops courage by doing courageous acts.
—Aristotle

What do you think this saying means?

_____

_____

ACTIONS: BEING SOMEONE'S HERO

List 5 ways you are a hero.

EXAMPLE:

I shoot hoops with the eight-year-old across the street whenever I see him alone out playing in his driveway.

1. _____

2. _____

3. _____

4. _____

5. _____

DECISIONS: BEING A WORLD HERO

Write about what you would do if you were a World Hero. Would you wipe out world hunger and disease or ensure all of the Earth's creatures are safe? How would you do this—through some magic invention or formula? What is your greatest vision or plan for how you would do this? Who would you enlist for support and to help?

_____

_____

_____

_____

_____

_____

_____

Heroes are just regular folks with one exception: when someone needs help, they help.

—Anonymous

What does this quote mean to you?

_____

_____

How Your Brain Decides If You Will Become Addicted—Or Not

Information and Encouragement for Teens, with Stories by Teens and Young Adults
Jennifer Leigh Youngs, A.A. | Bettie B. Youngs, Ph.D., Ed.D.

- *"using," dependency and addiction*
- *if you or a friend can't stop using*
- *Withdrawal, Relapse, and Recovery*
- *cool ways to say "no"*

Book: 978-1-940784-99-1
e-book: 978-1-940784-98-4

Setting and Achieving Goals that Matter to ME

Information and Encouragement for Teens, with Stories by Teens
Jennifer Leigh Youngs, A.A. | Bettie B. Youngs, Ph.D., Ed.D.

- *discovering what's important TO ME*
- *hobbies, talents, interests, apptitudes*
- *hopes, aspirations and dreaming big*
- *my goal-setting workbook*

Book: 978-1-940784-97-7
e-book: 978-1-940784-96-0

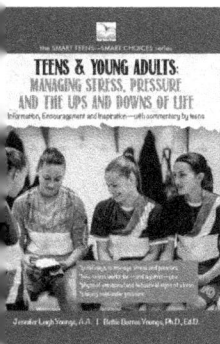

Managing Stress, Pressure, and the Ups and Downs of Life

Information, Encouragement and Inspiration—with commentary by teens
Jennifer Leigh Youngs, A.A. | Bettie B. Youngs, Ph.D., Ed.D.

- *great ways to manage stress and pressure*
- *how stress works for—and against—you*
- *physical, emotional and behavioral signs of stress*
- *staying cool under pressure*

Book: 978-1-940784-80-9
e-book: 978-1-940784-81-6

The 10 Commandments and the Secret Each One Guards—For You

Information and Inspirational Short Stories
Bettie B. Youngs, Ph.D., Ed.D. | Jennifer Leigh Youngs, A.A.

- *how the Commandments speak to you*
- *the secret each Commandment guards*
- *using your faith to guide the choices you make*
- *how to be confident and bold in your faith*

Book: 978-1-940784-95-3
e-book: 978-1-940784-94-6

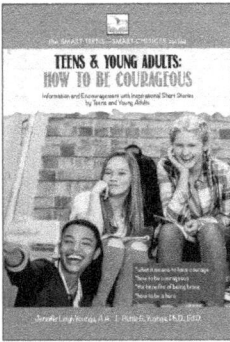

How to Be Courageous

Encouragment and Inspirational Short Stories by Teens and Young Adults
Jennifer Leigh Youngs, A.A. | Bettie B. Youngs, Ph.D., Ed.D.

- *the importance of being courageous*
- *the benefits of being brave*
- *how to be a hero*

Book: 978-1-940784-93-9
e-book: 978-1-940784-92-2

Growing Your Confidence and Self-Esteem

Information, Encouragement and Inspirational Short Stories by Teens and Young Adults
Jennifer Leigh Youngs, A.A. | Bettie B. Youngs, Ph.D., Ed.D.

- *being on good terms with YOU*
- *feeling "good enough"*
- *the power of confience*
- *liking the face in the mirror*
- *being happy and "forward looking"*

Book: 978-1-940784-86-1
e-book: 978-1-940784-87-8

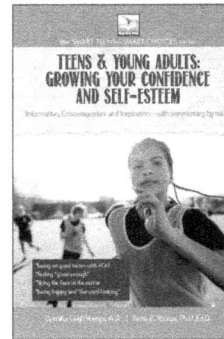

Faith at Work in Our Lives

Information, Encouragement and Inspirational Short Stories by Teens and Young Adults
Jennifer Leigh Youngs, A.A. | Bettie B. Youngs, Ph.D., Ed.D.

- *talking faith with your friends*
- *faith as an anchor in your life*
- *accepting and caring for others*
- *faith in victories and defeats*

Book: 978-1-940784-78-6
e-book: 978-1-940784-79-3

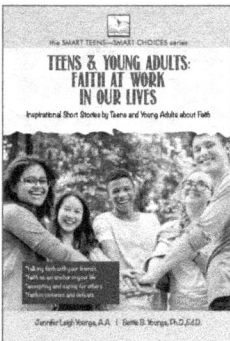

Understanding Feelings of Love

Inspirational Short Stories by Teens and Young Adults
Jennifer Leigh Youngs, A.A. | Bettie B. Youngs, Ph.D., Ed.D.

- *the lessons of love*
- *setting boundaries important to you*
- *4 ways to be a great boy/girlfriend*
- *when love relationships end*

Book: 978-1-940784-75-5
e-book: 978-1-940784-74-8

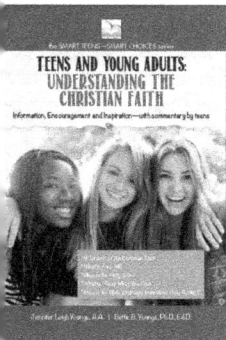

Understanding the Christian Faith

Information, Encouragement and Inspirational Short Stories by Teens and Young Adults
Jennifer Leigh Youngs, A.A. | Bettie B. Youngs, Ph.D., Ed.D.

- *9 Tenants of the Christian Faith*
- *What is Free Will*
- *What is the Holly Spirit*
- *What is "Reap What You Sow"*
- *How is the Bible as unique from other Holy Books?*

Book: 978-1-940784-76-2
e-book: 978-1-940784-77-9

How to be a Good Friend

Information and Encouragement with Inspirational Short Stories
by Teens and Young Adults
Jennifer Leigh Youngs, A.A. | Bettie B. Youngs, Ph.D., Ed.D.

- *understanding friendships*
- *how to be a good friend*
- *making, keeping, and ending friendships*
- *mending hurt feelings*

Book: 978-1-940784-73-1
e-book: 978-1-940784-72-4

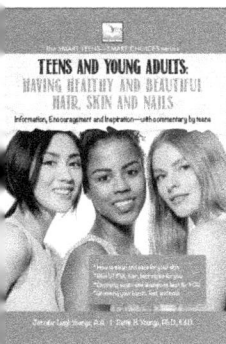

Having Healthy and Beautiful Hair, Skin and Nails

Information, Encouragement and Inspiration—with commentary by teens
Jennifer Leigh Youngs, A.A. | Bettie B. Youngs, Ph.D., Ed.D.

- *how to clean and care for your skin*
- *BEAUTIFUL hair; best styles for you*
- *choosing soaps and shampoos best for YOU*
- *grooming your hands, feet, and nails*

Book: 978-1-940784-84-7
e-book: 978-1-940784-85-4

The Power of Being Kind, Courteous and Thoughtful

Information, Encouragement and Inspirational Short Stories by Teens and Young Adults
Jennifer Leigh Youngs, A.A. | Bettie B. Youngs, Ph.D., Ed.D.

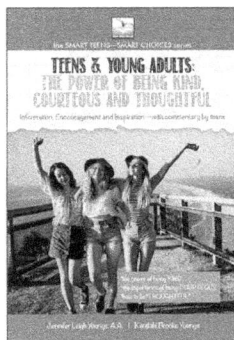

- *the power of being KIND*
- *the importance of being COURTEOUS*
- *how to be "THOUGHTFUL"*

Book: 978-1-940784-82-3
e-book: 978-1-940784-83-0

How to Have a Great Attitude
Information, Encouragement and Inspirational Short Stories by Teens and Young Adults
Jennifer Leigh Youngs, A.A. | Bettie B. Youngs, Ph.D., Ed.D

- *food—your body's source of energy*
- *sleep—restores body and brain*
- *liking the face in the mirror*
- *stress, anxiety, and emotional ups and downs*

Book: 978-1-940784-90-8
e-book: 978-1-940784-91-5

Caring for Your Body's Health and Wellness
Information, Encouragement and Inspirational Short Stories by Teens and Young Adults
Jennifer Leigh Youngs, A.A. | Bettie B. Youngs, Ph.D., Ed.D.

- *food—your body's source of energy*
- *sleep—restores body and brain*
- *liking the face in the mirror*
- *stress, anxiety, and emotional ups and downs*

Book: 978-1-940784-88-5
e-book: 978-1-940784-89-2

TEEN TOWN PRESS
www.TeenTownPress.com

www.BettieYoungsBooks.com
info@BettieYoungsBooks.com

AVAILABLE ON-LINE
and from the
INGRAM BOOK COMPANY

Bettie Youngs Publishing Co., Inc.
www.BettieYoungsBooks.com
info@BettieYoungs.com

Foreign Rights:
Sylvia Hayse Literary Agency, LLC
hayses@caat.com

www.ingramcontent.com/pod-product-compliance
Lightning Source LLC
Chambersburg PA
CBHW021342090426
42742CB00008B/706